Katie
SWaRts

Now I Know

Birds

Written by Susan Kuchalla
Illustrated by Gary Britt

Troll Associates

Library of Congress Cataloging in Publication Data

Kuchalla, Susan.
  Birds.

  (Now I know)
  Summary: Simple text and illustrations introduce
some of the common and individual characteristics of
a variety of birds.
  1. Birds—Juvenile literature. [1. Birds]
I. Britt, Gary, ill. II. Title.
QL676.2.K83   598   81-11412
ISBN 0-89375-656-3   AACR2
ISBN 0-89375-657-1 (pbk.)

What is a bird?

There are many kinds of birds. There are robins, bluejays, and owls . . . to name a few.

There are many colors of birds.

A cardinal is red.

A starling is black. A goldfinch is yellow.

There are also many sizes of birds.
A hummingbird is very small.

An eagle is very big.

An ostrich is even larger.

All birds have feathers.

The feathers help them fly.

And the feathers also keep the birds warm.

All birds hatch from eggs.

The eggs are many colors and sizes.
A robin's egg is blue and small.

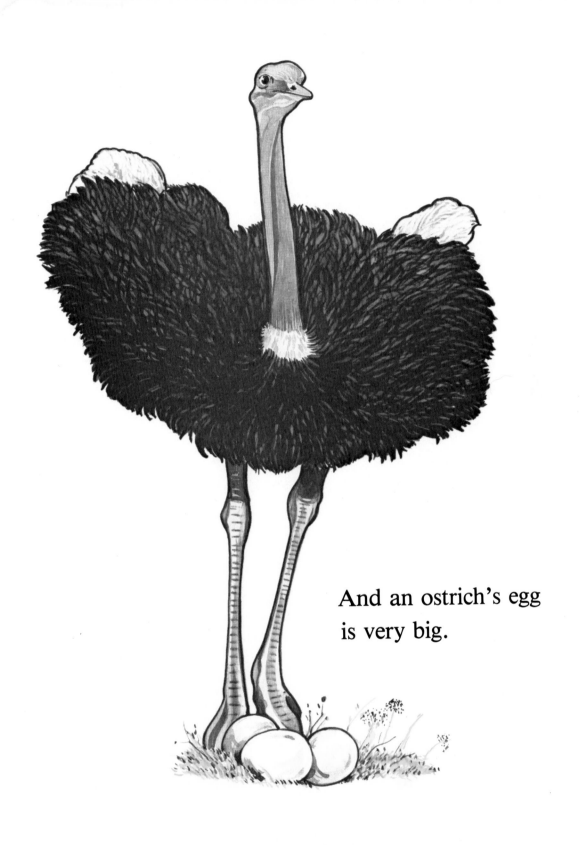

And an ostrich's egg
is very big.

Many birds make nests for their eggs.

They start with a few twigs and leaves.

And they hold it all together with mud.

The father bird watches the nest.

The mother bird keeps her eggs warm.

And soon they are ready to hatch.

Crack! The baby birds are born!

Baby birds are very hungry.

The mother and father are very busy finding food.

Baby birds eat many times a day.

They grow very fast.

Soon they are ready to leave the nest.

They flap their wings and fly away.

They are big birds now.

One day they will make a nest of their own.